DON'T MAKE ME FLY

BY ELAINE A. POWERS

ILLUSTRATED BY NICHOLAS THORPE

Don't Make Me Fly

by Elaine A. Powers
Copyright 2017 by Elaine A. Powers
All rights reserved.

ISBN-13: 978-1547150304
ISBN-10: 1547150300

Published by Lyric Power Publishing LLC, Tucson AZ 2015

All information provided is believed and intended to be reliable, but accuracy cannot be guaranteed by the author or the publisher.

DON'T MAKE ME FLY

By Elaine A. Powers

Illustrations by Nicholas Thorpe

Roadrunners run here, there, they prefer not to fly,
Roadrunners run everywhere, and I'll tell you why.
Their wings are too weak for flying around,
But their legs are strong for running on ground.
They live to run, hunting for prey to seize.
They run up the trees, looking for bees.

They run over rocks looking for toads.
In fact, roadrunners ran before there were roads!

Though they are known to prefer desert land,
They inhabit places other than sand.
They thrive in grasslands, creosote, and mesquite,
Life in pinyon-juniper woods is also a treat.
Roadrunners need open spaces to roam.
Dense forests or cities are not good homes.

Though they don't fly well, roadrunners can glide,
If frightened, they will sail a short distance to hide.
They can flap a short ways to perch on a tree,
But only if that is where they really need to be.

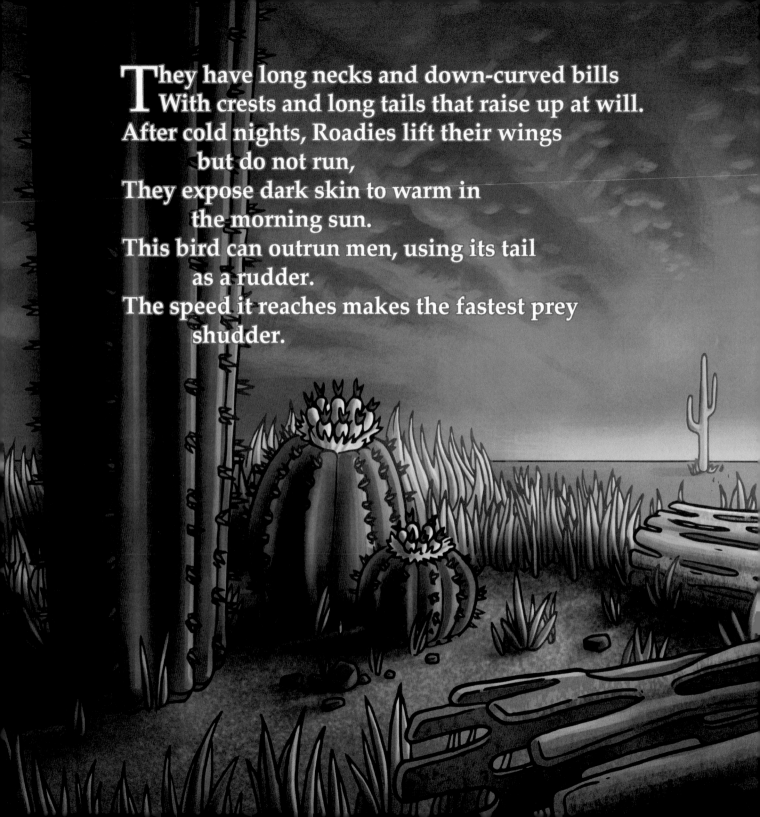

They have long necks and down-curved bills
  With crests and long tails that raise up at will.
After cold nights, Roadies lift their wings
        but do not run,
They expose dark skin to warm in
        the morning sun.
This bird can outrun men, using its tail
        as a rudder.
The speed it reaches makes the fastest prey
        shudder.

Reptiles, mice, birds, insects, anything small
The roadrunner eagerly eats them all.
Spreading their wings like a feathery cape,
Spiraling in, they prevent the prey's escape.
Catching venomous critters takes special skill,
Yet, Roadies who eat them never get ill.

They grab
their victim
behind its head,
And bash it on
the ground until it
is dead.

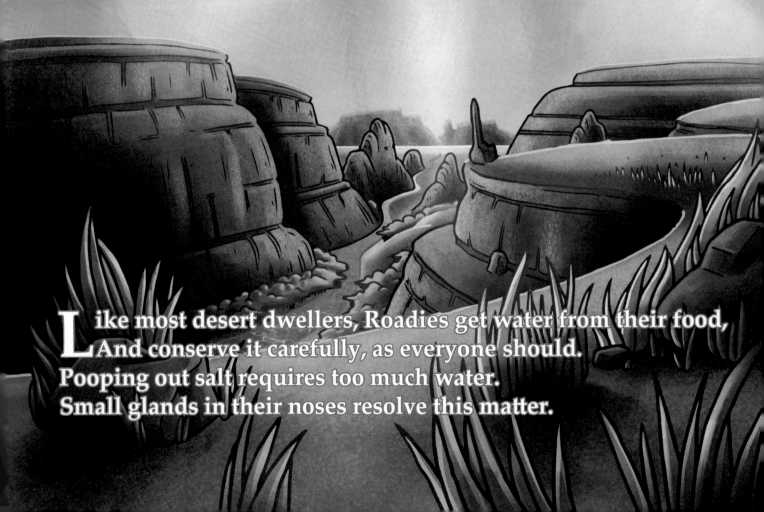

If a meal is too long, the bird
lets it protrude.
Not finishing it would be
considered quite rude.
The Roadie wanders around,
swallowing a bit at a time.
A long-lasting entrée can be the
best kind to find.

Horned lizards can also be
tricky to eat.
Spikes must face out if
Roadie's heart is to beat.
Roadies use speed to run
down ground prey,
Or leap, grabbing insects
or hummers that don't
get away.

Like most desert dwellers, Roadies get water from their food,
And conserve it carefully, as everyone should.
Pooping out salt requires too much water.
Small glands in their noses resolve this matter.

Native Americans have great respect for this bird,
Tales of their speed, strength and courage are heard.
Some say they're sacred and must not be killed,
Others say the meat with energy is filled.

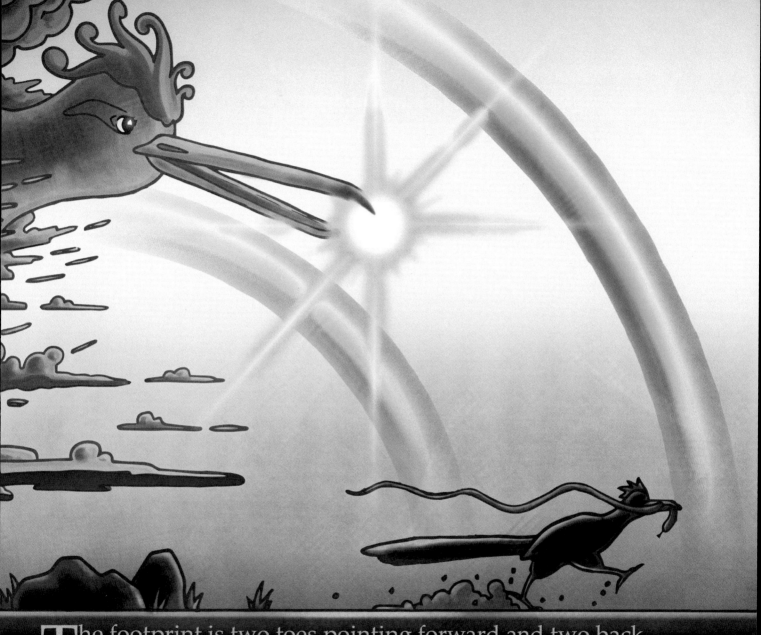

The footprint is two toes pointing forward and two back,
Making which way they are running difficult to track.
This X, a sacred symbol, hides their direction from showing.
This prevents following evil spirits from knowing.

When a Roadie finds a potential mate,
He offers her a bite of food as bait.
The female will take it, if satisfied,
Consenting to be his roadrunner bride.

Twigs are laid in a bush tall and cozy,
To keep eggs safe from those who are nosy.
Both parents take turns warming the nest,
But at night, the heat from father is best.

Up to twelve eggs are laid, early hatchlings
　　do best.
The chicks who emerge first often
　　　crowd out the rest.
The parents catch prey to feed their brood.
The biggest chicks beg the loudest,
　　　getting more food.
A few weeks later, fledglings go out
　　　on their own,
Leaving their parents, to explore and roam.

There are dangers to Roadies that can't be concealed.
Hawks, raccoons and coyotes find them a filling meal.
Roadrunners use their speed to get away,
Living to run around yet another day.

Raising the crest is an assertive guise,
That exposes orange-red spots near the eyes.
Legend says these spots are from stealing fire,
But they're a sign that the situation is dire.

Roadrunners' lives are affected by man.
Disturbing their habitat should be banned.
The land is changed and provides no support
And house cats feel killing them is really great sport.

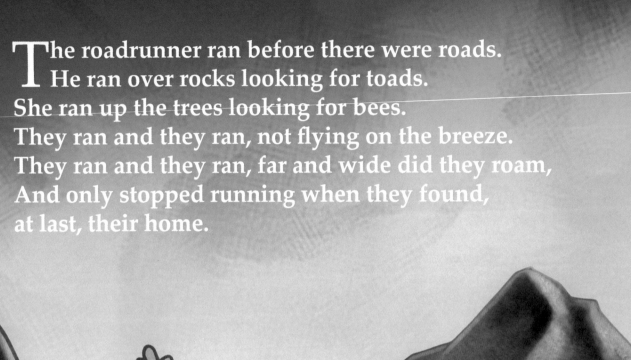

The roadrunner ran before there were roads.
He ran over rocks looking for toads.
She ran up the trees looking for bees.
They ran and they ran, not flying on the breeze.
They ran and they ran, far and wide did they roam,
And only stopped running when they found,
at last, their home.

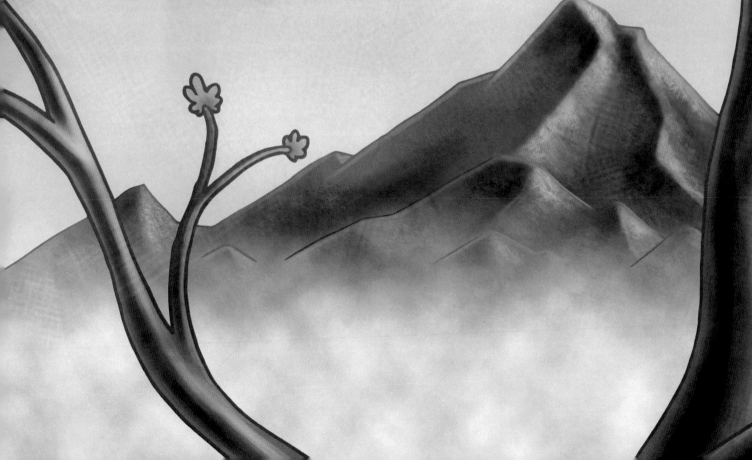

ACKNOWLEGMENTS:

I'm grateful to those who helped me create this book: Pamela Bickell, Brad Peterson, and Kate. J. Steele for their critical reading; my indispensable editors Annie Maier and Nora Miller; and my illustrator Nick for bringing the text to life. I'd also like to express my appreciation to the roadrunners of my neighborhood who inspired me.

Made in the USA
Las Vegas, NV
29 December 2021

39784886R00017